THE OPENING

Beloved: *Opening Your Heart, Part I,* is a six-lesson Bible study that lays a strong foundation for our true identity as beloved daughters of God.

Unshaken: *Opening Your Heart, Part II,* is a six-lesson Bible study that fills our spiritual toolbox with exactly what we need to grow stronger in our faith.

Steadfast: *Opening Your Heart, Part III,* a six-lesson Bible study, unpacks why we are hustling for our worth and how to conquer our fears.

THE KEEPING IN BALANCE SERIES

Harmony: Keeping in Balance, Part I
Perspective: Keeping in Balance, Part II
Exhale: Keeping in Balance, Part III

THE DISCOVERING OUR DIGNITY SERIES

Tapestry: Discovering Our Dignity, Part I
Legacy: Discovering our Dignity, Part II
Heritage: Discovering Our Dignity, Part III

For more information on all Walking with Purpose Bible studies please visit us at
walkingwithpurpose.com

walking with purpose

walking with purpose

Dear Friend,

Please receive this little booklet as a gift with this message: You are loved and treasured by God.

You may already know that, or you might doubt it with every fiber of your being. Regardless, God says *come*. He won't ask you to clean up first or hustle to prove your worth. He simply invites you to slow down and give a little time to your heart and your spiritual life.

The ability to carve out even a few minutes to nurture your spirit is a challenge. We get it. So we felt called to put together this sample of our inspiring Bible study series *Beloved. Unshaked. Steadfast.* It includes some of our favorite life-changing lessons and we hope you'll consider it a token of God's affection for you.

Don't overwhelm yourself by thinking that Bible study is a huge commitment. Just set a small goal and see what you can do in a month. Give God a little bit of time each day as you move through these insightful lessons.

I promise you, He will not be outdone in generosity. He never is.

With prayers for you as you open your heart to the One who loves you best ~

Lisa Brenninkmeyer
Founder and Chief Purpose Officer, Walking with Purpose

Opening Your Heart Series
Sample Booklet

www.walkingwithpurpose.com

Authored by Lisa Brenninkmeyer
Cover and page design by True Cotton
Production management by Christine Welsko

IMPRIMATUR   + William E. Lori, S.T.D., Archbishop of Baltimore

Any Internet addresses (websites, blogs, etc.) in this book are offered as a resource,
and may change in the future. Please refer to www.walkingwithpurpose.com as the
central location for corresponding materials and references.

Printed: February 2018

ISBN: 978-1-943173-10-5

Opening Your Heart Series Sample Booklet

Opening Your Heart Series Sample Booklet

TABLE OF CONTENTS

INTRODUCTION

SAMPLE LESSONS

APPENDICES

These sample lessons have been taken from our three-part Bible study, *Opening Your Heart* series. For a full listing of the topics covered in these Bible studies, please see page number 3.

Opening Your Heart Series I, II, III

TOPICS

Beloved – Series I

Abba ~ God the Father

Emmanuel ~ Jesus Christ

No Longer Slaves ~ Friendship with Jesus

Surge of the Heart ~ Prayer

Sweet Guest of the Soul ~ The Holy Spirit

Grace ~ The Difference Maker

Unshaken – Series II

Fight Like a Girl ~ The Battle Is Real

Filled to Overflow ~ We Need the Eucharist

Embraced by Mercy ~ We Need Reconciliation

Our Refuge ~ We Need a Mother

Saturated in Scripture ~ We Need God's Word

Never Alone ~ We Need Our Church

Steadfast – Series III

Worthy ~ Owning Your Identity

Lionhearted ~ Conquering Your Fears

Unshackled ~ Experiencing Real Transformation

Valiant ~ Suffering with Purpose

Welcomed Home ~ Receiving Forgiveness

Empowered ~ Reading the Bible

Welcome to Walking with Purpose

You have many choices when it comes to how you spend your time – thank you for choosing to try Walking with Purpose. Studying God's Word with an open and receptive heart will bring spiritual growth and enrichment to all aspects of your life, making every moment that you've invested well worth it.

Each one of us comes to this material from our own unique vantage point. You are welcome as you are. No experience is necessary. Some of you will find that the questions in this sample booklet cause you to think about concepts that are new to you. Others might find much is a review. God meets each one of us where we are, and He is always faithful, taking us to a deeper, better place spiritually, regardless of where we begin.

The Structure of *Opening Your Heart* Series Sample Booklet

Opening Your Heart Series Sample Booklet is a Bible study that includes two of our favorite lessons from our three-part *Opening Your Heart* series: *Beloved, Unshaken* and *Steadfast.* Each study is six weeks long and all integrate Scripture with the teachings of the Roman Catholic Church. Formatted to encourage daily time spent in the Bible, each lesson points to principles that help us manage life's pace and pressure while living with calm and steadiness.

This booklet is designed to give you a taste of our life-changing Bible studies through interactive personal study. We hope you enjoy it!

Sample Booklet Format and Reference Materials

Opening Your Heart Series Sample Booklet is divided into two sections:

The first section comprises two lessons. The lessons are divided into five "days" to help you form a habit of reading and reflecting on God's Word regularly. If you are a woman who has only bits and pieces of time throughout your day to accomplish tasks, you will find this breakdown of lessons especially helpful. Each day focuses on

Scripture readings and related teaching passages, and ends with a Quiet Your Heart reflection. In addition, Day Five includes a Saint's Story; a lesson conclusion; a resolution section, in which you set a goal for yourself based on a theme of the lesson; and short clips from the *Catechism of the Catholic Church (CCC),* which are referenced throughout the lesson to complement the Scripture study.

The second section, the appendices, includes an article about Saint Thérèse of Lisieux, the patron saint of Walking with Purpose (Appendix 1). Appendix 2 is the article "Conversion of Heart". Appendix 3 is the answer key. You will benefit so much more from the study lessons if you work through the questions on your own, searching your heart, as this is your very personal journey of faith. The answer key is meant to provide personal guidance or insight when needed.

The Bible
The recommended Bible translations for use in Walking with Purpose studies are: The New American Bible, which is the translation used in the United States for the readings at Mass; The Revised Standard Version, Catholic Edition; and The Jerusalem Bible.

Walking with Purpose™ Mission Statement

Walking with Purpose aims to bring women to a deeper personal relationship with Jesus Christ by offering personal studies and small group discussions that link our everyday challenges and struggles with the solutions given to us through the teachings of Christ and the Roman Catholic Church.

About the Author

Lisa Brenninkmeyer, raised as an evangelical Protestant, entered the Catholic Church in 1991. She has led Bible studies in Europe, Mexico, and the United States, and has written curricula for women and children. She founded Walking with Purpose in 2008 out of a desire to see women come to know Christ personally. Her speaking and writing are inspired by a desire to see women transformed as they realize how much God loves them. She holds a BA in psychology from St. Olaf College. She lives with her husband, Leo, and their seven children in St. Augustine, Florida.

Lessons

NOTES

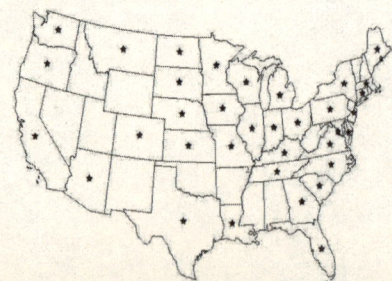

Walking with Purpose is a community of women growing in faith – together! This is where women are gathering. Join us!

www.walkingwithpurpose.com/find-program-near

Lesson 1

WORTHY ~ OWNING YOUR IDENTITY

Introduction

Her Instagram feed painted a picture of a successful, carefree, full life. Keeping her eye out for "moments" and incorporating white space to give her feed room to breathe made all the difference. If you measured the quality of her days by the beauty depicted on the screen, you'd say she was nailing it. But behind her camera and well-curated public image, she was miserable. She wasn't the only one feeling this way, but few would admit it out loud.

The pressure to hustle for our worth is felt professionally, socially, and even spiritually. At work or school, we want to impress people with our skills, knowledge, intellect, and creativity. We're told that we have to come up with an elevator pitch that communicates all we have to offer—a verbal résumé—and to be ready to share it instantly and winsomely. The concept of personal branding makes us wonder what makes us so special. Deep down, we worry we aren't.

We know we're supposed to have a full social calendar. We wonder if we're filling our time with things we actually enjoy, or if we're just committing to things in order to avoid being alone. The silence of alone time can be scary, because then the questions about our worth, the confusion about what we're doing with our lives, and the insecurities of relationships start to crowd our minds. We want people and activities to distract us from questions that don't seem to have answers.

Our spiritual lives aren't immune to this kind of pressure, either. It's so hard to say, "I am enough. I have done enough." Most of us have some faulty thoughts regarding what kind of a father God is. Lies abound around His love. Even when we've taken time to get to know God personally, the desire to perform for Him in order to earn His love can seep in.

Is there another way to live?

Oh, my friend, there most certainly is. And it is *good*. Freedom can be found if we are willing to let go of habits that keep us shackled. But we'll need to learn to listen to God's voice more intently than we listen to people's opinions. At first, this new way of living might feel awkward. That's an inevitable part of change. But then it will start to feel OK, and ultimately, it will feel like the release and breath of fresh air that we are longing for.

The first step is acknowledging that we have been lied to. Our culture has convinced us to measure our worth by the wrong things. So many of these lies *feel* true, and we have unconsciously embraced them. We need to name them—to bring these false ways of determining our value into the light. Then we need to compare them to what *God* says.

Each day of this lesson, we'll explore one of these destructive lies and compare it to our God-given, true identity. Archbishop Fulton Sheen said, "The truth is the truth even if no one believes it, and a lie is a lie even if everyone believes it." This means that there are some lies that a lot of people believe, and sorting through them all can be confusing. But we are promised in John 8:32 that we *can* know the truth, and *the truth will set us free.*

Day One
THE LIE: MY WORTH IS DETERMINED BY WHAT I LOOK LIKE AND WHAT I DO

THE TRUTH: MY WORTH IS ROOTED IN MY IDENTITY AS A CHERISHED DAUGHTER OF GOD

1. A. List some messages that our culture sends to women in terms of their worth. As you read the list, do any of these messages regularly mess with your mind? If so, which ones?

B. The author of Psalm 139 had a healthy sense of self-worth. Read Psalm 139:13–15, and record the ways he described himself. Do these words reflect your self-image?

2. A. What do we learn from 1 Samuel 16:7 about the difference between how God sees us and how people measure our worth?

B. What labels have people given you throughout your life? Do you feel boxed in by them? Have you started using these words or labels to describe yourself?

Seeing yourself through the eyes of God doesn't happen automatically. It requires that you be intentional about what you allow to saturate your mind. If this is an area of struggle for you, check where your time goes. Whose voice is getting more airtime in your head—God's words about your worth found in Scripture, or definitions of what is desirable and beautiful found on the Internet?

I find it interesting that the Bible doesn't try to convince us that achievements and appearance don't ever matter. It paints an accurate picture about how the world works, but then draws us toward a mind-set that values God's opinion over man's.

In the book of Esther, the most attractive, alluring, and charming virgins in the country are brought together so the king can try them out and pick a new wife. Their dignity is about to be stripped away, but before they are to be paraded before him, they need to receive beauty treatments—which should cause us to pause and say, "*What?* Weren't these the most beautiful young women in the country?" What was true then is true now. By the world's standards, we'll never be gorgeous enough. There will always be someone prettier and thinner. Beauty is a multibillion-dollar business. Society tells us, "You are only as valuable as you are beautiful," and we are offered product after product to help us become more "valuable."

But our worth isn't measured in the mirror. It's been measured at the cross. And you have already been measured and considered worth *everything* to Jesus. In the words of author and speaker Mark Hart, "You have a God who loves you so much, He would rather die than risk spending eternity without you." His love for you has nothing to do with your outward beauty. It has everything to do with your heart, which is irresistible to Him.

3. A. According to Titus 3:4–5, what had *no bearing* on Jesus' decision to die for us? Which aspects of His character caused Him to make this sacrifice?

B. How did He save us (Titus 3:5–6)? He saved us so that what would happen (Titus 3:7)?

C. What state were we in when Jesus saved us? See Romans 5:8.

We're justified by His *grace*—not by our list of accomplishments, personal brand, portfolio, qualifications, or perfection. Jesus decided we were worth dying for and offered us His grace when we were still messed up and falling short of our potential. He invites us to draw near and hear Him whisper, "Beloved," when we are at our worst. No matter what we do or don't do, our worth in His eyes is unchanging. God loves us not because *we* are good, but because *He* is good.

4. A. Because of Jesus, through faith and our baptism, what is our new identity? See Galatians 3:26.

B. Whom did God send as proof of our adoption as His children? What are we now to call God? See Galatians 4:6.

14

5. Read Romans 8:14–16 and describe what it means to be adopted children of God.

Quiet your heart and enjoy His presence. . . .

Being led by the Holy Spirit is an indicator that we are daughters of God. Does this mean that whenever we aren't led by the Holy Spirit we stop being God's children? Does our identity falter when we are weak and fail? No. But it does mean that if we are going to act like who we really are, we need to seek guidance from the Holy Spirit, and do what He tells us to do. Being "led by the Spirit" may sound a little ethereal and hard to grasp. We don't need to overcomplicate this. What do you sense that God wants you to do right now? There will always be some areas where we're confused and unsure, but there is usually some clarity around an area where we'd rather do things our own way. Romans 8:14 reminds us that a daughter of God recognizes that she is not her own, that she was purchased for a price on the cross, and that she should go where God is telling her to go. But as a beloved daughter, she trusts that even if it isn't the plan she prefers, it's ultimately for her benefit.

One thing is certain: A daughter of God has no need to fall back into fear. As she grows in trusting God, His love for her, and His consistent delivery on all His promises, fear starts to lose its grip on her heart.

Unlock the fullness of life through gratitude. Take a few minutes to reflect on what it cost Jesus for you to have a new identity as a beloved daughter of God. Thank Him for His unfailing love, described in Jeremiah 31:3: "I have loved you with an everlasting love; I have drawn you with unfailing kindness." Thank Him for loving you more than His own life, and for being unchanging.

Day Two
THE LIE: I NEED A SIGNIFICANT OTHER TO VALIDATE MY WORTH.

THE TRUTH: I AM COMPLETE IN CHRIST.

1. A. It is the most natural and normal thing in the world to want to be chosen and desired. The alternative—being passed over, dismissed, or rejected—can wound us deeply. Take a moment and look back on your life. When was the first time you experienced disapproval or rejection in a powerful enough way that it led you to question your worth?

   B. What does John 15:16 reveal about how wanted you are?

You are chosen. This truth flies in the face of any sense of inadequacy, all insecurities, and every bit of self-doubt. It delivers the news that no matter who has rejected you, no matter how many times you've received the message that you are not enough, that you are lacking in some way, God chose you, because you are precious to Him. You are wanted. You were made by a God who knows your name, who marked you as His. You belong. You are chosen. Ponder this truth for a moment. Let it sink into your mind and heart, traveling to memories and current places of rejection. Allow His relentless, personal love for you to overpower the self-diminishing thoughts.

Because the truth is, too often we don't take the time to pause and reflect on our true worth and how beloved we are. A painful interaction occurs, the feelings of rejection get shoved down as we try to ignore them, and then we go in search of something or someone to make us feel better. This rarely, if ever, gives us the deep sense of worthiness that we long for.

We really get ourselves into trouble when we expect a man to give us that sense of worth or to fill up what we feel is lacking within us. All too often, we don't know that this is what we are doing. We just have an overwhelming sense that we need a boyfriend or a husband, and that being single is somehow less than being in a relationship.

This actually sets any current or future boyfriend or husband up for failure. There is no way that any person can fill the place in our hearts that is meant for Christ alone. We also are tempted to compromise on qualities that we should look for in someone with whom we are willing to share our hearts.

In Colossians 2:10, we are given an important truth to declare over our lives: *"I am complete in Christ."* This means that He is enough to fill what feels empty. That missing piece of the puzzle of our lives? It's *Him*.

2. What are we challenged to do in Proverbs 4:23?

When you connect deeply with a guy—physically or emotionally—you don't walk away from that relationship unaltered. There's something called "heart glue," and when you separate, you leave a little piece of yourself with that person, and it can really hurt. Maybe you have felt that in your own life.

Proverbs 4:23 calls our heart "the wellspring of life." Another word for *wellspring* is *source*. This means that your heart is the source of your life. If your heart stops beating, you stop living. That's the physical side of it. Emotionally, it's where our feelings dwell.

Our hearts matter to God, and only He can satisfy our longings. Only God will be perfectly tender with our hearts. People in our lives will make mistakes and disappoint at some point. Only God will love us unfailingly with a steadfast, faithful, and merciful love. But He'll never completely satisfy us if we keep looking for someone else to fill us up. He's a gentleman. He won't force His way into our hearts.

3. It's natural to want a person with flesh and bones to comfort and care for us. There's nothing wrong with turning to people with our needs. But it would be such a game changer if we learned to turn to God first. We can't see God, but we can hear His voice. Write out the following verses and underline them in your Bible. These are your love notes from God.

When you feel ugly → Song of Songs 4:7

When you feel alone → Isaiah 41:10

When you feel unlovable → Isaiah 43:4

When you feel insignificant → Isaiah 49:15–16

When you feel afraid → Psalm 34:8

When you need to know someone cares → Psalm 56:9

When you feel angry → Exodus 14:14

When you feel stupid → 1 Corinthians 1:27–29

When you need a hero → John 14:1–3

Quiet your heart and enjoy His presence. . . . God has a beautiful plan for your life.

Meditate on the following adaptation of the prayer Be Satisfied with Me, by St. Anthony of Padua:

Everyone longs to give themselves completely to someone,
To have a deep soul relationship with another,
To be loved thoroughly and exclusively.
But to a Christian, God says, "No, not until you are satisfied,
Fulfilled and content with being loved by Me alone,
With giving yourself totally and unreservedly to Me.
With having an intensely personal and unique relationship with Me alone.
Discovering that only in Me is your satisfaction to be found,
Will you be capable of the perfect human relationship,
That I have planned for you.
You will never be united to another
Until you are united with Me.
Exclusive of anyone or anything else.
Exclusive of any other desires or longings.
I want you to stop planning, to stop wishing, and allow Me to give you
The most thrilling plan existing . . . one you cannot imagine.
I want you to have the best. Please allow Me to bring it to you.
You just keep watching Me, expecting the greatest things.
Keep experiencing the satisfaction that I am.
Keep listening and learning the things that I tell you.
Just wait, that's all. Don't be anxious, don't worry
Don't look around at things others have gotten
Or that I have given them
Don't look around at the things you think you want,
Just keep looking off and away up to Me,
Or you'll miss what I want to show you.
And then, when you're ready, I'll surprise you with a love
Far more wonderful than you could dream of.
You see, until you are ready, and until the one I have for you is ready,
I am working even at this moment
To have both of you ready at the same time.
Until you are both satisfied exclusively with Me
And the life I prepared for you,
You won't be able to experience the love that exemplified your relationship with Me.
And this is perfect love.
And dear one, I want you to have this most wonderful love,
I want you to see in the flesh a picture of your relationship with Me.

And to enjoy materially and concretely the everlasting union of beauty, perfection and love that I offer you with Myself.
Know that I love you utterly. I am God.
Believe it and be satisfied."[1]

Day Three
THE LIE: I NEED PEOPLE'S APPROVAL TO BE HAPPY.

THE TRUTH: I CAN LIVE FOR AN AUDIENCE OF ONE.

This is a lie that does contain some truth, so it's easy to believe. The truth is, it's easier to be happy when people approve of us. But we don't *need* their validation. And if our choices are too influenced by what others think of us, we'll definitely be tempted to compromise.

If we want to grow closer to God, then it's worth pausing to take a look at what motivates our behavior. Ideally, we're motivated by a pure love for God. But in the lives of most women, the opinion of others is a primary motivator. Instead of seeking security and value in God, we look for other people to measure our worth. As a result, our actions are driven by our desire for affirmation, to be noticed, and to be praised: "I'll do, so I can be loved." There is a difference between liking to be appreciated and doing something in order to be appreciated. In the latter case, our value is determined by the opinions of others. We become people-pleasers, motivated more by what those around us want than by what God is calling us to do and be.

The greatest need of a woman who is driven by others' opinions of her is to be loved. Out of a fear of rejection, we define ourselves by how other people perceive us. God calls us to define ourselves by His unconditional love for us. When we settle for the fickle love of other people, it's harder for us to soak up God's love. Ideally, we'll be so filled up with His love that it can spill over into the lives of those around us, helping us to love as Christ loves. But when we're obsessed with what others think of us, we often struggle to have intimate relationships. Our greatest concern is to be affirmed and validated, and so the temptation is enormous to wear a mask and be whoever we think those around us want us to be.

---

[1] "Be Satisfied with Me," The Practicing Catholic, http://thepracticingcatholic.com/2015/06/13/be-satisfied-with-me/ (accessed September 6, 2017).

Oftentimes, when we recognize that we are motivated by others' opinions of us, we find that some of this has come from our relationships with our earthly fathers. If our earthly fathers don't love us unconditionally and communicate that effectively, we will often, as young girls, seek that affirmation from friends. As we get older, we'll seek it from a boyfriend and later, from a husband. In these relationships, we are seeking security. We are seeking affirmation that we are worthy of love. When this is what drives us, we desperately need God's unconditional love to fill us.

1. A. What instructions are we given in 1 Corinthians 16:13?

We have to be on our guard, because our ability to deceive ourselves is sky-high. Unless we're slowing down and asking ourselves hard questions, we'll fail to look at what is motivating our behavior. Paying attention to which people and places tempt us to slip on a mask will help alert us to times when we're probably tempted to compromise who we truly want to be.

We need to stand firm in the faith. As we encounter people whose beliefs differ from ours, we are always to respect where someone else is coming from. At the same time, we need to remain rooted in what we know to be true. If we have tied people's approval to our sense of well-being, it'll be hard to stand firm in the faith. Many followers of Christ feel too Christian for one group and too secular for another. This causes people to feel they don't belong anywhere, which can be pretty unsettling. It requires courage and strength to stand alone.

B. Have you experienced the ache of not belonging? Has the desire to fit in ever tempted you to compromise what you believe? Can you identify any relationships that make it hard for you to courageously stand firm? Share your story here.

2. Poet and activist Maya Angelou wrote, "You are only free when you realize you belong no place—you belong every place—no place at all. The price is high. The reward is great."[2]

I invite you to read that quote again, this time more slowly. At first glance, this might make you think that if she's right, freedom is impossible to achieve. Because who can get rid of the deep desire to belong? What does she mean? How can we belong everyplace and no place at all?

Please hear me on this: I am in no way suggesting that the desire to belong is wrong. I believe it is hardwired within us. The ache to belong is so familiar to me. . . . It makes me think of a memory of all my friends making me walk home from school on the other side of the street because I had danced with the wrong boy during PE in sixth grade. Then countless memories of betrayal by a high school boyfriend whom I had trusted with my heart come to mind, and it still stings. I remember a social event where everything was riding on my winning the approval of the women there. I gave it my best shot, paying attention to my clothes and my facial expressions and my words, but backs literally turned after I was looked up and down with disapproval. After decades of being Catholic I still feel like there is an "inner club" that I will never belong to because I grew up Protestant and am a woman. I have spent decades of my life in pursuit of the holy grail of belonging, and the price I've paid for compromise is too high to count.

Freedom from this way of living . . . oh, this I want. Do you? I think it's worth exploring what Maya Angelou was describing. It has everything to do with learning how to *live for an audience of One*. But even as I read that, I know how easy it would be to think, "OK, so God's opinion is the one that really matters. So I need to perform well for Him." To that, I say an emphatic *no*. We do *not* perform for God.

In trying to flesh out the true meaning of what I'm getting at, a quote from Scottish Olympic athlete and missionary Eric Liddell comes to mind. His words were made famous by the film about his life, *Chariots of Fire*: "God made me fast. And when I run, I feel His pleasure."

How did God make you—your unique personality, passions, and abilities? Which convictions are nonnegotiable for you?

---

[2] Maya Angelou, "A Conversation with Maya Angelou," interview by Bill Moyers, *Bill Moyers Journal*, PBS, November 21, 1973.

As God watches you, it gives Him the most enormous pleasure when you run *your* race, remaining true to who you really are. If you will allow His pleasure to be your deepest motivator, you'll begin to experience a sense of deep belonging when you are being your true self—the woman God created you to be.

3. A. According to Philippians 3:20, where do we belong?

   B. Citizenship denotes membership in a community. How is that community described in Hebrews 12:1?

   C. What is the "great cloud of witnesses" watching us do?

Who are these people described in Hebrews 12:1? They are the great spiritual athletes of the past. It's the communion of saints, the people who have gone before us to heaven and are now cheering us on as we run toward the finish line. It's the people in the Hebrews 11 Hall of Faith: Noah, Abraham, Moses, Rahab, David, Samuel, the apostles . . . all these people who lived through the beatdown of running their race and ended in victory. They are looking at you and saying, "I did it—and so can you! Run your race!"

Hebrews 12 is filled with this imagery of a race being observed. The great cloud of witnesses aren't the only ones there watching. Who else is there as you run? Who is your home team, your tribe? You need at least one person who is there when you fall, who knows how to both commiserate and commission. This is the person who says, "You're right, that really was awful. You really choked. Yeah, it actually was that bad. But you showed up. And that is what matters. That is what counts. You showed courage because that is who you are. You are a courageous warrior— a spiritual athlete—and you are going to get back in the race. I am here to help you to get there." These are the people who really matter, the flesh-and-blood people who are there for you in the low moments and celebrate with you in the high ones. Lean in to these people. Listen to their words. Don't act as if their words don't matter because they already like you. And don't tell them that you are fine when you are not. Lean in. They are one of God's greatest gifts to you.

D. Which person in your life encourages you to show up as your truest self, picks you up when you fall, and speaks words of life to your heart?

Quiet your heart and enjoy His presence. . . . Picture His smile of pleasure as He looks at you, His beloved daughter.

As you run your race, there will always be critics in the arena. You can learn to anticipate their comments and acknowledge their presence, but never make their approval your goal. Look to the great cloud of witnesses for encouragement, and cultivate a "home team" of friends who call out your truest, best self.

But there is One who should have the very best seat in the arena. He has been there Himself and experienced the beatdown of all beatdowns. He gets what it feels like to be shredded and to keep going. The critics? He had hordes of them, and their cruelty surrounded Him when He was at His weakest. His opinion is the one that matters most. In fact, in the end, His is the only one that will count. We are to run with our eyes fixed on Him.

We are to give Him *the best seat in the arena, and never, ever take our eyes off Him.*

It's scary to step out into the arena and embrace the life that we were created to live. It involves training and has a cost. We aren't promised that this marathon will be easy. But we are promised that in the end, we will be face-to-face with the One who has been sitting in the arena all along saying, "Lock your eyes on mine! You can do it! You can walk this path! I went there ahead of you and experienced far worse. And do you know why I did it? So that I could be with you. I did it all for you, for this incredible time when I can welcome you home and bring you into a rest that is like nothing you have ever experienced!"

Fix your eyes on Jesus and become who you were designed to be—the daughter of the King, full of the greatness and glory of your Father. Lift up your head, and run your race.

Day Four

THE LIE: MY SENSE OF WORTH WILL BE HIGHER IF I PUT MYSELF FIRST.

THE TRUTH: MY SENSE OF WORTH INCREASES IN PROPORTION TO MY SELF-GIVING.

"It's not selfish to do what's best for you."

"Fall in love with taking care of yourself."

"Personal branding got you down? Follow these five easy steps to create clarity and confidence!"

"I'm all about me. My growth, my goals, my happiness, my worth."

For some of us, reading those quotes makes us nod our heads in agreement. We're determined not to be doormats or passed over. Aren't these supposed to be the best years of our lives?

For others, they scream of self-centered, superficial living. Saint Teresa of Calcutta's words come to mind: "A life not lived for others is not a life."

Many of us read these quotes and think they take it a little far, but that self-care has got to factor into the way we live.

Where's the balance? What's the truth?

1. A. What insight do we gain from Jesus in Matthew 6:31–33?

These verses remind me that the problem isn't whether or not my outfit is fashionable. Wearing something ugly or outdated doesn't make me holy, and wearing something cute doesn't make me sinful. What Jesus is pointing out is our tendency to get preoccupied and worried about superficial things. First things first: He asks that our main focus be God's kingdom and our righteousness.

In his book *Making All Things New*, Henri Nouwen puts it this way:

Jesus does not respond to our worry-filled way of living by saying that we should not be so busy with worldly affairs. He does not try to pull us away

25

from the many events, activities, and people that make up our lives. He does not tell us that what we do is unimportant, valueless, or useless. Nor does he suggest that we should withdraw from our involvements and live quiet, restful lives removed from the struggles of the world.

Jesus' response to our worry-filled lives is quite different. He asks us to shift the point of gravity, to relocate the center of our attentions, to change our priorities. Jesus wants us to move from the "many things" to the "one necessary thing." It is important for us to realize that Jesus in no way wants us to leave our many-faceted world. Rather, he wants us to live in it, but firmly rooted in the center of all things. Jesus does not speak about a change in activities, a change in contacts or even a change of pace. He speaks about a change of heart. This change of heart makes everything different, even while everything appears to remain the same. This is the meaning of "set your hearts on his kingdom first . . . and all these other things will be given you as well." What counts is where our hearts are. When we worry, we have our hearts in the wrong place.[3]

Take some time to think about Nouwen's words, then read Matthew 6:21. As you reflect on these teachings, where do you think your treasure is? Where is your heart? In other words, what is at the center of your attention?

B. What do you think it means to seek something *first?* What might look different in your life if you re-arranged your priorities regarding where you spend your time and put God's kingdom and your righteousness first?

One practical way to look at the word *first* is to think about the way we start the day.

What do we grab first? The phone or the Bible?

Whom do we talk to first? Our friend or God?

---

[3] Henri Nouwen, *Making All Things New* (New York: HarperCollins, 1981), 17.

Where do we look for the day's schedule first? The calendar or the guidance of the Holy Spirit?

I'm not suggesting that we ignore a schedule or never make a to-do list. But I do think it helps us set our priorities when we look at our calendars *while* talking to the Lord, letting Him know that these events and commitments are what we think matter most, but that we recognize He may have a different plan. Starting the day with this attitude can help us view inevitable interruptions as divine appointments.

2. What insights do you gain from the following New Testament verses about a life of self-sacrifice?

Matthew 6:24–25

John 12:24–25

Philippians 3:8

3. Sometimes what discourages us from a life of self-giving is a feeling that the little we can do doesn't make much of a difference. If it isn't Instagram-worthy, we can be tempted to think it doesn't matter. It's also easy to be overwhelmed by the tremendous needs around us. We might think to ourselves, "I'm not Mother Teresa. I can't begin to address the major things that are wrong in the world." All too often, because we can't do something great, we just binge-watch Netflix.

If our saint of Calcutta were sitting with us, I wonder how she'd respond. Let's let her speak for herself. Read the following quotes by Mother Teresa, and journal your thoughts. Does one quote stand out to you? Do you feel convicted? Motivated?

"We know only too well that what we are doing is nothing more than a drop in the ocean. But if the drop were not there, the ocean would be missing something."[4]

"Do not think that love in order to be genuine has to be extraordinary. What we need is to love without getting tired. Be faithful in small things because it is in them that your strength lies."[5]

---

[4] "Quotes About Ocean," Goodreads, https://www.goodreads.com/quotes/tag/ocean (accessed September 27, 2017).

"In this life we cannot do great things. We can only do small things with great love."[6]

"At the end of life we will not be judged by how many diplomas we have received, how much money we have made, how many great things we have done. We will be judged by 'I was hungry, and you gave me something to eat, I was naked and you clothed me. I was homeless, and you took me in.'"[7]

"Do not wait for leaders; do it alone, person to person."[8]

"If you are humble nothing will touch you, neither praise nor disgrace, because you know what you are."[9]

A. My thoughts:

B. If you could help one group of people in the world, whom would it be and what would you do?

Quiet your heart and enjoy His presence. . . . You cannot outgive God.

Hardwired into each of our souls are "longings for the infinite and for happiness" (CCC 33). According to the Catechism, this "desire [for happiness] is of divine origin: God has placed it in the human heart in order to draw man to the One who alone can fulfill it: We all want to live happily; in the whole human race there is no one who does not assent to this proposition, even before it is fully articulated" (CCC 1718).

This is a good, holy, and God-given desire. But we get ourselves in trouble when we seek to have that desire satisfied in superficial ways. Unfortunately, sometimes we gain just enough pleasure that we

---

5 "Mother Teresa Quote," Great-Quotes.com, http://www.great-quotes.com/quote/141903 (accessed September 27, 2017).

6 Quotationsbook, http://quotationsbook.com/quote/24701/ (accessed September 27, 2017).

7 Goodreads, https://www.goodreads.com/quotes/759-at-the-end-of-life-we-will-not-be-judged (accessed September 27, 2017).

8 Goodreads, https://www.goodreads.com/quotes/12081-do-not-wait-for-leaders-do-it-alone-person-to (accessed September 27, 2017).

9 Goodreads, https://www.goodreads.com/quotes/55677-if-you-are-humble-nothing-will-touch-you-neither-praise (accessed September 27, 2017).

stop seeking deeper fulfillment and satisfaction. Our focus turns inward, and our perspective can quickly grow dark and hopeless. It's as our focus turns outward that light rushes into our souls, filling us with the perspective we need to remain grateful at all times and suffer well when that is required.

When we make our self-worth the highest good or our main focus, we will not experience the fullness of life we were created for. The abundant life is found in self-giving.

In the words of Saint John Paul II:

> *It is Jesus that you seek when you dream of happiness; He is waiting for you when nothing else you find satisfies you; He is the beauty to which you are so attracted; it is He who provoked you with that thirst for fullness that will not let you settle for compromise; it is He who urges you to shed the masks of a false life; it is He who reads in your heart your most genuine choices, the choices that others try to stifle.*

> *It is Jesus who stirs in you the desire to do something great with your lives, the will to follow an ideal, the refusal to allow yourselves to be ground down by mediocrity, the courage to commit yourselves humbly and patiently to improving yourselves and society, making the world more human and more fraternal.*[10]

Take a few moments to quiet down and listen for the Holy Spirit's guidance. Is He asking you to shed a mask? To let go of some things that are preoccupying you and taking up too much of your time? Do you need to ask the Lord for courage to overcome some fears? Talk to Him about His plans for your life. His plans are for your good—to prosper and not to harm you, to give you a future full of hope (Jeremiah 29:11). Offer Him your best, your all. You will not be disappointed.

"Perhaps you were born for such a time as this." (Esther 4:14)

Day Five
SAINT'S STORY

Saint Catherine of Siena

How did an uneducated woman in the Middle Ages grow to be so influential that Pope Gregory XI not only listened to her, but did what she said? This powerful

---

[10] Goodreads, https://www.goodreads.com/author/quotes/6473881.Pope_John_Paul_II (accessed September 26, 2017).

figure, Saint Catherine of Siena, was truly remarkable and intriguing. She was born in 1347 in Siena, Italy, and from childhood, she had visions of Christ and an unusual intimacy with Him, the Virgin Mary, and the saints in heaven. A true mystic, Saint Catherine lived in the realm of the spiritual, connecting heaven and earth in her day-to-day life. Although she never studied theology, she is a Doctor of the Church, meaning her teachings are for the whole Church. She's considered a teacher for the ages.

Her life of extreme asceticism (she was so committed to fasting that she hardly ate anything) and her otherworldly visions might make you believe that people thought she was crazy. When she prayed, she entered a state of such ecstasy that she was totally unresponsive to anyone or anything around her, not even wincing when a needle was put in her hand. But the people who were honored and respected during the medieval period were of a different sort than the individuals we honor in our culture. The most respected men and women were those who were in touch with the sacred. Most important, Saint Catherine's life was so exemplary—sacrificial, pious, and devout—that her good character and overall wisdom made it impossible to consider her insane. Her life was looked at in its entirety, and she shone among all others as a standout—a leader, a witness, a saint. Caring for the sick (especially during the black plague) and going where no one else wanted to serve revealed her self-forgetful love for all.

Saint Catherine of Siena lived during a time when the pope was living in Avignon, France, instead of Rome. The Church was falling into financial and moral ruin, and Saint Catherine believed that the key to its survival was for the pope to return to Rome. So at age twenty-eight, she traveled to Avignon, got an audience with the pope (her reputation preceded her), and convinced him to return to the Eternal City. She remained committed to Pope Gregory and his successor in Rome, Pope Urban VI, until her death.

Quotes and teachings of Saint Catherine of Siena continue to inspire us today, regardless of how many years ago they were spoken. Our hearts are stirred when we read her words, "Be who God meant you to be and you will set the world on fire." She believed this wholeheartedly, and knew that our ability to live this radically and impact the world so significantly would require a high level of self-forgetfulness. Our obsession with putting our best face forward on social media is quite a contrast to the kind of living she recommended. "What is it you want to change?" Saint Catherine asked. "Your hair, your face, your body? Why? For God is in love with all those things and he might weep when they are gone."[11] To Saint Catherine of Siena, all that

---

mattered was what her Beloved thought of her. His love was intoxicating, consuming, and more than enough to deeply satisfy her.

Saint Catherine of Siena suffered, as all the saints have. Instead of running from it, she welcomed it as an opportunity to strip away self-preoccupation and focus her mind and heart fully on Jesus. Her union with Jesus was worth everything. She truly experienced a mystical marriage with Christ. Before you write this off as an experience reserved for the spiritual giants, I assure you, it isn't something set aside only for the saints. Jesus took on human flesh and came to us all seeking intimacy. This is what He desires with you and me. In Saint Catherine's words, "We are of such value to God that He came to live among us . . . and to guide us home. He will go to any length to seek us, even to being lifted high upon the cross to draw us back to Himself. We can only respond by loving God for His love."[12]

In Matthew 10:39, Jesus says, "Whoever finds his life will lose it, and whoever loses his life for my sake will find it." Saint Catherine of Siena lost herself in Christ, and in doing so, she found the deepest fulfillment, intimacy, belonging, and joy. Her abandonment to God's will allowed her to trust Him utterly and say, "He will provide the way and the means, such as you could never have imagined. Leave it all to Him, let go of yourself, lose yourself on the cross, and you will find yourself entirely."[13]

What can we do to keep a balance between healthy self-care and self-centeredness? In what way would you like to grow in self-forgetfulness?

Conclusion

We long for concrete purpose and direction in life. The last thing we want is to feel we are floating around with no vision for the future. Living in the land of "what if's" can be incredibly unsettling, and we feel so much more *worthy* when we know we are doing what God made us to do. This desire to discover our vocations is normal and good. But before we can discern our vocation– our mission in life– we need to be rooted in our true identity as daughters of God. This must come first or we'll run the risk of living as human *doings* instead of human *beings*. When we discover our true worth as unconditionally loved daughters, we can rest in the reality that nothing we do can earn more or less of God's love.

---

[12] Ibid.
[13] Ibid.

The Catholic Church teaches that there are three primary vocations: married life, the priesthood, and consecrated life. All of these vocations are related to our roles in life and our callings. Our secondary vocation is the unique way in which we use our God-given gifts and talents to help others.

Discovering our primary and secondary vocations requires discernment and patience. If we are going to live intentionally, we should put in the time to identify our specific callings, but we need to be careful that we never allow our work or ministry to define us. When we lose ourselves in a role or a calling and connect our performance to our identity, we'll forfeit the steadiness and confidence that is our birthright as daughters of God. God's approval is the only one that matters. He is calling us to step out into a broken world with giving hearts, not counting numbers or comparing size of mission, but simply showing up and loving sacrificially.

Perhaps you know exactly what God has called you to, exactly where He wants you to be serving. If your vocation is clear, know that you are truly fortunate. Most young women (and older ones as well, actually) aren't sure exactly what they are being called to do. It isn't a matter of not wanting to make a difference or being unwilling to serve. There's just a lack of clarity regarding the where and the what.

Do you know that when God created you, He also created a specific work that you are expected to do? There are certain tasks with your name on them that God wants you to accomplish. Ephesians 2:10 says that "we are God's handiwork, created in Christ Jesus to do good works, that God prepared in advance for us to do."

The key is identifying what those good works are. God has planted seeds in your soul—seeds of discontent. When you see something in the world that you just can't stand, that may be one of the things He wants you to do something about. Truly, miracles happen when a young woman says, "I just can't stand this anymore," and turns to God for guidance. When you feel anger, righteous indignation, frustration, and compassion welling up in you, turn to God and ask Him, "Is this it? Is this one of the things that you created me to do something about?" At some point in your life, you will find that one thing, that stirring of passion that God has placed in your heart.

There are a myriad of things that aren't right around us, but what is the one issue, the one group of people, the one thing that really gets you worked up? It doesn't matter if it's something you figure is too big for you to solve. What is it that grabs your heart? That breaks your heart? That gets you up off the couch saying, "Something has got to be done about that"?

Perhaps it is something connected to an experience of suffering in your life. Please know that none of your tears of pain will be wasted by God. He can use every ounce of what you have been through to make this world a better place. In 1 Corinthians 1:4 we are taught that God "encourages us in our every affliction, so that we may be able to encourage those who are in any affliction with the encouragement with which we ourselves are encouraged by God."

Whatever heartache you have been through has uniquely equipped you to step out and minister to people going through the same thing. There is such a difference between someone saying, "I'm sorry," and someone saying, "I understand, because I've been there." Past trauma shouldn't define us, but it can equip us for life-changing ministry and impact.

In his book *Holy Discontent*, Bill Hybels writes: "I assure you, there is a holy discontent with your name on it. There is something out there that God is waiting for you to grab on to so that he can use you to help solve it. It wrecks you, it wrecks him and he's ready for you *both* to do something about it."[14]

Together, you can set the world on fire.

My Resolution

"My Resolution" is your opportunity to write down one specific, personal application from this lesson. We can take in a lot of information from studying the Bible, but if we don't translate it into action, we have totally missed the point. In James 1:22, we're told that we shouldn't just hear the Word of God; we are to "do what it says." So what qualities should be found in a good resolution? It should be **personal** (use the pronouns *I, me, my, mine*), it should be **possible** (don't choose something so far-fetched that you'll just become discouraged), it should be **measurable** (a specific goal to achieve within a specific time period), and it should be **action oriented** (not just a spiritual thought).

Examples:

1. I struggle to see myself the way God sees me. To help renew my mind, I will memorize 1 Samuel 16:7 ("God does not see as a mortal, who sees the appearance. The LORD looks into the heart.") or Song of Songs 4:7 ("You are beautiful in every way, my friend, there is no flaw in you."), so the Holy Spirit can bring this verse to my mind when I am feeling bad about myself.

---

[14] Bill Hybels, *Holy Discontent* (Grand Rapids, MI: Zondervan, 2007), 54.

2. I feel like I wear a mask with so many of my friends. I will either determine to be real with a carefully chosen few, or find a new friend whom I can trust with my heart. Either way, I will step out of my comfort zone and take a risk to be real.

3. I will go to adoration and ask God to help me take a look at times in my life when I have suffered. I will ask Him if there is someone He wants me to reach out to so that I can offer comfort as someone who has "been there." Then I will follow through, reaching out to that person with a phone call, text, or an offer to get together.

My resolution:

Catechism Clips

CCC 33 The *human person*: with his openness to truth and beauty, his sense of moral goodness, his freedom and the voice of his conscience, with his longings for the infinite and for happiness, man questions himself about God's existence. In all this he discerns signs of his spiritual soul. The soul, the "seed of eternity we bear in ourselves, irreducible to the merely material," can have its origin only in God.

CCC 1718 The Beatitudes respond to the natural desire for happiness. This desire is of divine origin: God has placed it in the human heart in order to draw man to the One who alone can fulfill it:

> We all want to live happily; in the whole human race there is no one who does not assent to this proposition, even before it is fully articulated.

> How is it, then, that I seek you, Lord? Since in seeking you, my God, I seek a happy life, let me seek you so that my soul may live, for my body draws life from my soul and my soul draws life from you.

> God alone satisfies.

Lesson 2

LIONHEARTED ~ CONQUERING YOUR FEARS

Introduction

The storms of the rainy season in Guadalajara, Mexico, were powerful and breathtakingly intense. The kids loved it when we'd take our Suburban out in the midst of a storm. They'd scream with excitement as the water broke over the hood of the car and splashed on their windows, climbing up the sides of the car. Smaller cars would start to float around the roads, out of control. The sensible thing would have been to stay home, but we loved the thrill of being out in the middle of it all, and we had (somewhat groundless) confidence in our Suburban's ability to stay steady no matter what. Our kids liked the rain and the sense of adventure that the storms would bring.

At least that was the case until one particularly crazy storm. We were all at home, enjoying the afternoon, when the rains began. Five-year-old Amy was playing in her bedroom and I was reading in the living room. Bedrooms were on one side of the house, the kitchen on the other, and the two-story, open living room was in the middle with skylights covering most of the ceiling. The rain started calmly enough, but all of a sudden, noises began to explode as hail pelted the skylights. There was a crack, and as I looked up to see the skylights shattering and raining down shards of glass everywhere, Amy appeared at the doorway of her bedroom. Terrified, she began to run through the flying glass to get to me.

And I froze.

I froze. What kind of a mother *freezes* at a time like that? The same mother who knows the Heimlich maneuver yet froze when her three-year-old was choking on a marble. Thank heavens someone with a cool head was nearby to help. I don't know why on earth that has been my reaction not once, but twice, and thank the Lord our brave babysitter was in the kitchen and ran through the glass to rescue Amy. But fear can do that. It can be utterly paralyzing at the absolute worst times imaginable.

Not surprisingly, Amy wasn't so fond of rain after that. And like clockwork, we could count on a daily storm during the rainy season. My response was to comfort her and hold her, to play music loudly during the storms to drown out the sound of the rain. Her daddy's approach was a little different. When the storm would start, he would scoop her up and take her outside. He'd ask her to look at his face, and then he'd smile and talk about how much he loved the rain. He'd stomp in the puddles and make it all a game. Little by little, as she'd watch his lack of fear and total comfort in the storm, she got to the point where she would stomp in the puddles herself. Fear didn't get the last word.

Jesus desires that peace rule in each of our hearts. Yet many people live paralyzed by fear. Panic attacks are on the rise; in any given year, about one-third of American adults have at least one. Sometimes one can see the effects of fear in people in the form of phobias or fearful behavior. But more often, we hide our fears in our hearts. Sometimes even our best friends don't know our secret fears, but they are there, robbing us of the joy that Jesus wants each of us to experience every day. During this lesson, we'll explore ways we can conquer our fears, allowing them to come under the control of God's loving hand.

Day One
AFRAID OF THE STORM

The emotion of fear is a gift insofar as it alerts us to danger. Our senses become heightened, and we look for a way out. Fear lets us know the storm is coming or has hit, but it's not enough to get us *through* the storm. We need something more than that.

Read Matthew 14:22–33.

1. What shift in focus caused Peter to start sinking in the waves? How was he saved from drowning?

2. What kind of a spirit has God given us? See 2 Timothy 1:7.

A spirit of fear will alert us to danger and sharpen our senses, but it will never provide us with what we need to navigate the storms of life. To make it through those circumstances, we need supernatural power, God's unconditional love, and the self-control that helps us choose to dwell on certain things and not others. The good news is, this is exactly what the indwelling Holy Spirit provides. If we replace our spirit of fear with the Spirit of power, love, and self-control, we can conquer our fears.

3. In what ways have you seen God's power in your life? When have you experienced His unconditional love? Has He ever strengthened you by helping you to have self-control in an area of weakness? Share your experiences here and let God's track record of faithfulness increase your confidence in Him. Whatever you face, His presence within you will make all the difference.

Quiet your heart and enjoy His presence. . . . Allow God to dispel your fear.

Fear is unavoidable, but what we choose to do with it is up to us. In the very moment that we feel afraid, we can remind ourselves, "God has not given us a spirit of cowardice but rather of power and love and self-control." (2 Timothy 1:7) That is what is inside us.

When panic hits, grab hold of Jesus' hand. Lock your eyes on the truth that you are not alone, that He is present, and that His presence makes all the difference. Ask Him to dispel your fear.

"You who dwell in the shelter of the Most High, who abide in the shade of the Almighty, say to the Lord, 'My refuge and fortress, my God in whom I trust.'" (Psalm 91:1–2)

"I learned that courage was not the absence of fear but the triumph over it. The brave man is not he that doesn't feel afraid, but he who conquers that fear." —Nelson Mandela

Day Two
AFRAID OF WALKING ALONE AT NIGHT

A survey conducted by Chapman University, in California, discovered that one of Americans' greatest fears is walking alone at night.[15] When people answered the survey, they were probably thinking of the dark alley, the dimly lit parking lot—that sort of thing. I understand this fear. Once the sun goes down, I imagine someone is hiding under my car in the mall parking lot, just waiting to slash my ankles. I start to regret that my hair is always in a ponytail because that's easy for some ne'er-do-well to grab. I walk with my finger over the alarm button on my key fob because you just never know. So I get being freaked out at night.

Night can mean all that—or it can be a metaphor for a general darkness in our circumstances or a darkness in our souls. And we are very afraid of walking through those times alone. That's when walking with your hair down and the key fob in hand just doesn't offer much comfort. So what does Scripture have to say to that fear? Let's dive in. There are lots of verses to look up today, friends. But hang with me. You might end up discovering a couple that you'll carry with you from now on.

1. Did Jesus promise that if we follow Him, He'll remove all challenges from our lives? See John 16:33.

2. What did Saint Teresa of Ávila learn from her experience of trusting God in every circumstance? See CCC 227.

3. Look up the following verses. What does each teach you about walking through darkness?

   A. Deuteronomy 31:6

---

[15] Jolie Lee, "Biggest American Fear? Walking Alone at Night, Survey Finds," *USA Today*, October 22, 2014, http://www.usatoday.com/story/news/nation-now/2014/10/22/fear-study-chapman-university/17663861/.

B. Psalm 27:1 and John 8:12

C. Isaiah 41:10

D. Romans 8:28

4. Which of these verses helps you the most in dealing with your fears? Write it down on an index card and carry it with you.

Quiet your heart and enjoy His presence. . . . God does His finest work in the darkness.

"God has to work in the soul in secret and in darkness because if we fully knew what was happening and what Mystery, transformation, God and Grace will eventually ask of us, we would either try to take charge or stop the whole process." —Saint John of the Cross

The deepest soul work is done in the darkness, and it isn't a group exercise. There are times when God allows us to go to places that we wouldn't choose to go, because it is only there that we will be transformed in the most beautiful of ways. But we shouldn't be afraid of this, because God accompanies us there. We never walk in darkness alone. True, we may feel alone. But our feelings don't define reality. God does. And He promises never to leave us. He is there in the secret places in a way that our minds don't really comprehend.

Take the verse you chose for question 4 and personalize it. Turn it into a prayer of thanksgiving. For example, using Isaiah 41:10, you could pray:

Dear Lord,

Thank you for making it so that I do not need to be afraid, because you are with me. I don't need to be anxious, because you are my God. Thank you for strengthening me. Thank you for helping me. Thank you for upholding me with your victorious right hand. Thank you for grasping hold of me and never letting me go.

Day Three
AFRAID OF REJECTION

We don't always recognize this as a personal struggle because we don't connect the fear of rejection with its fruits. This fear manifests itself as people-pleasing, approval seeking, a heightened sensitivity to criticism, feelings of worthlessness, and a rejection of others so that we turn away before they do. We need to get to the root of this fear if we want to walk in freedom.

1. How does Proverbs 29:25 describe "fear of man" or "fear of others"? Note: The phrase used in the Bible to describe being a people-pleaser or caring too much what others think of us is "fear of man."

A snare is a trap that typically has a noose of wire or a cord. Caring too much what others think is a snare that strangles our freedom. It causes us to crave approval and fear rejection, and puts people in a place meant for God alone.

2. We all experience rejection at some point in our lives. It's unavoidable. But being afraid of it or totally train wrecked by it is actually optional. It all boils down to what our identity is based on. If the way our worth is defined is through people's acceptance of us, then fear of rejection will always be a noose around our necks. But if we can totally embrace the truth that **people's opinions do not determine our worth or identity, that our worth is determined by God and our identity is rooted in being His beloved daughter**, then freedom can be ours.

God's approval is the only one that ultimately matters, and He *adores you*. Yes, *you*. You are not an exception to the rule, no matter what you've done or what you're struggling with today.

What insight do the following verses give as we seek to please God and find our identity in Him?

Romans 8:31

Galatians 1:10

Colossians 3:23

3. Do you struggle with a fear of rejection? If so, in what specific way? (Typical manifestations of this fear are people-pleasing, approval seeking, sensitivity to criticism, feelings of worthlessness, tendency to reject others.)

Quiet your heart and enjoy His presence. . . . Do you want God to show up in your life in a powerful way? Are you tired of the status quo and ready for more? Would you like to see God, in all His glory, intersect your circumstances?

God wants us to experience His glory. He wants to pour out His power on us and to see us living freed, transformed lives. This has always been His desire. When Jesus walked the earth, there was nothing He wanted more—for the people to see His glory and to be changed as a result. But so many of them missed it. Why? The reason is found in the Gospel of John: "For they preferred human praise to the glory of God" (John 12:43). They wanted something more than God's power and glory. They wanted human praise.

Jesus is turning to you now and asking, "What do you want?" How will you answer Him?

Day Four
AFRAID TO LEAN IN TO JOY

"What if I fall?
Oh, my darling, what if you fly?"[16]

1. Jesus came to set us free from the fears that hold us back from soaring as God's beloved daughters. How is the life He desires for us described in the following verses?

John 10:10

---

[16] Erin Hanson, "Just My Poems," The Poetic Underground,
http://thepoeticunderground.com/post/87639964775/the-talent-of-all-of-you-astounds-me-this-a-quote.

1 Timothy 6:17 (the second part of the verse)

Isaiah 30:18

These verses paint a picture of God wanting us to live deeply satisfying, meaningful, joy-filled lives. These are God's own words, so we can count on them as truth.

But how often do we believe the lies instead? All too often, we don't see God as a gracious, generous father. We believe the lie that He's going to hold out on us (this, of course, was the thought that got things spiraling out of control in the Garden of Eden). Some of us believe the lie that God is a disinterested father. Disaster might be just around the corner, but He's too busy with other things to do anything about it.

Believing lies about God really messes with our ability to embrace and live the life we were created for.

Have you ever realized that your life is going pretty well, and instead of resting in the joy of that moment and thanking God for all He's given, you think, "Oh, no! The other shoe is about to drop"? In her vulnerability research, Dr. Brené Brown has found that the most terrifying, difficult emotion we experience is *joy*. We're afraid to lean in to joy, because the thought of it being taken away is so scary. She describes our mental response as "dress-rehearsing tragedy":

> Dress rehearsing tragedy, she explains, is imagining something bad is going to happen when in reality, nothing is wrong. "How many of you have ever . . . [woken] up in the morning and thought, 'Oh my gosh, job's going great. Parents are good. This can't last.'"[17]

This isn't how God wants us to live. He wants us to lean in to joy and soar! So how do we do that? How can we break free of our tendency to pull back in fear and miss our lives because we are living in the gray?

---

[17] "Brené Brown: 'Joy Is the Most Vulnerable Emotion We Can Experience,'" *Huffington Post*, October 27, 2013, http://www.huffingtonpost.com/2013/10/18/brene-brown-joy-numbing-oprah_n_4116520.html.

2. Hidden in the meaning of the word "Eucharist" is one of the ways we can lean in to the joy we were created for. *Eucharist* means "thanksgiving." Practicing gratitude is one of the best ways to live a life of joy.

List an area of your life where you fear something that is currently wonderful going awry. What are you afraid of specifically?

Practice gratitude by listing all the things you are grateful for about that very area of your life.

It's up to you. You decide which of those lists you are going to dwell on. One will leave you paralyzed by the fear of "what if." The other will lead you to joy.

3. Underneath our reluctance to really embrace joy is the fear that we will fall. And consciously or not, we figure that the higher the place we're falling from, the more it will hurt. So we climb down from the peak of joy and sit in the middle ground of low expectations because it feels safer. And life passes us by.

I can't promise you that you will never fall or that life will never bring you pain. But God makes us promises in Scripture that should make an enormous difference in the way we live. In Deuteronomy 33:27, He promises, "The eternal God is your refuge, and underneath are the everlasting arms." Write that verse below. Think about it. Why does this truth matter? What difference does it make to you personally?

Quiet your heart and enjoy His presence. . . . The Lord is your refuge.

Have you whispered these questions?

"What if I fall?"
"What if I fall because of disappointment?"
"What if I fall because of tragedy?"
"What if I fall because I'm just not good enough?"

Lean in and listen, my friend. If you fall, God will catch you. It's as simple as that. He promises that underneath you, no matter what height you are falling from, His everlasting arms are there to catch you. What do we find at the end of our resources, the end of our dreams, the end of our hopes? We find God's mercy. We find God's graciousness. We find shelter from the storm.

That shelter is available to you right now. "He will shelter you with his pinions, and under his wings you may take refuge" (Psalm 91:4). Come under His wings in prayer. Rest in safety.

"Because he clings to me I will deliver him; because he knows my name I will set him on high. He will call upon me and I will answer, I will be with him in distress; I will deliver him and give him honor. With length of days I will satisfy him, and fill him with my saving power." (Psalm 91:14–16)

Rest in these promises.

Don't miss your life.

Day Five
SAINT'S STORY

Blessed Anne of Saint Bartholomew, Saint Frances Xavier Cabrini, and Saint Joan of Arc

What God is asking of us—to cast our fears aside and follow Him, and to become saints and bring His message of hope to everyone around us through word, deed, and example—is too much for us. The funny thing is that He knows we can't do this without His help. He said it a long time ago: "I am the vine, you are the branches. Whoever remains in me, with me in him, bears fruit in plenty; for *cut off from me you can do nothing*" (John 15:5). When we experience fear in our pursuit of God's purpose for our life, it's because we are forgetting about that. Almost always, our fears are the result of depending too much on ourselves and not trusting enough in God, who is so powerful that He can turn even the most bitter failures (Christ's death on the cross) into the most glorious victories (Easter Sunday). Jesus put it concisely: "For men, it is impossible, but not for God, because everything is possible for God." The more we think about God's omnipotence and love, the more we fill our imagination with His goodness and the wonders He has done in so many lives throughout history, the more easily we will be able to overcome our fears and undertake the Christian adventure in which "the Spirit comes to the aid of our weakness" (Romans 8:26).

This was an especially difficult lesson for Blessed Anne of Saint Bartholomew. She came from a poor shepherding family in sixteenth-century Spain. As a Carmelite nun, Blessed Anne was sent to Belgium and France to start Carmelite convents, and to be prioress in some of them. She would often complain to our Lord that she was too ignorant and shy to be given such important responsibilities. In fact, she complained so much that finally He had to appear to her to calm her down. She had just tried to convince Him that He should choose someone else to do the work she was being asked to do, someone more intelligent, better educated, and more outgoing. So our Lord appeared to her and said, "It is with straw that I start my fires." He didn't comfort her by telling her how great she was. He simply wanted to do things in and through her, if she would let Him.

Saint Frances Xavier Cabrini, America's first canonized saint, illustrates this truth in a more down-to-earth way. She was born in Northern Italy in the 1800s. Early on, she experienced a strong desire to become a missionary, but no religious order would accept her because she had unstable health. So she gathered a group of companions and started her own religious order under the protection of her bishop. Soon she received approval from the pope and began her tireless apostolate with the poor Italian immigrants throughout the Americas. Her work required extensive travel between Europe and America. She ended up crossing the Atlantic more than thirty times on those clunky, uncomfortable, old-fashioned ocean liners. To do so, she had to overcome a mortal fear of water that she acquired after falling into a river and almost drowning when she was just a girl. That fear never left her; God never took it away. Even after years of sea travel, she declined an invitation from her sisters to go for a leisurely boat ride one day because she was afraid of the water! She told them, "I admit my weakness: I am afraid of the sea, and if there is no very holy motive in view, I have no courage to go where I fear danger."

Perhaps the most remarkable example of how trusting in God enables us to overcome fear is found in the truly amazing person of Saint Joan of Arc. A teenage girl, illiterate, of peasant stock, unable to ride horses, and unschooled in war, she received a call from God to liberate a divided and corrupt France from the overpowering and almost complete English invasion toward the end of the Hundred Years' War in the 1300s. No wonder she at first resisted the imprecations of the voices she heard (i.e. the saints whom God sent to her as His messengers)! They continually brought her God's message for four years before she finally obeyed when she was eighteen years old. It was only when they told her, "It is God who commands it," that she complied, entrusting herself completely to God's power. And the world has never been the same. She led armies, outfoxed evil courtiers, emboldened a cowardly king, revived an entire nation, and befuddled the most learned clerics and lawyers of her day. This illiterate teenager single-handedly reversed the fortunes of France and altered the history of Europe while enduring moral, physical, and psychological tortures of the cruelest kind. Through it all, she suffered profoundly, including confusion, exhaustion, and betrayal, ultimately being burned at the stake, dying with Jesus' name on her virgin lips.

And why? "It is God who commands it." She was able to do it because she *hoped in God*. She knew that serving God was her only true occupation, and that He would always be faithful to those who serve Him truly. Saint Joan of Arc left us a message: "Hope in God. Put your trust in Him, and He will deliver you from your enemies [fears]." Indeed, only God will never disappoint us; only He is worthy of our unbridled hope. When we feel helpless or fearful of all that Christ is asking of us, that's what we need to remember.

What fears are you facing in your life right now? How can Blessed Anne, Saint Frances, and Saint Joan of Arc inspire you to deal with them?

Conclusion

There hasn't been a moment of my life when I welcomed or sought out suffering. What I often forget is that it may be the very thing I need to experience in order to become the woman God wants me to be. Whenever I begin to think, "Surely, I shouldn't have to suffer since I try to do the right thing and live the way God wants me to," I think of the cross. It seems like the worst thing that could happen to anyone—defeat, humiliation, pain—but it was the ultimate victory and the accomplishment of our salvation.

So how do I conquer my fears? It's a journey. Sometimes it feels like two steps forward and one step back. But even then, progress is being made.

Because I'm so prone to fall back into fear, I frequently have to remind myself of the lessons contained in the points that follow. When fear starts to get the better of me, I go back to these lessons to readjust my thinking *and* my feelings:

Develop a mature view of suffering.

Because I live in a fallen world, I am quickly influenced by the world's view of the relationship between suffering and joy. We're told that they are polar opposites, but the truth is, there can be joy in suffering. When we meet God in the dark places and He gets us through, we can feel the joy of His presence. We can also feel joy when we realize that we are progressing spiritually as we face our fears, even when doing so is hard. A mature woman realizes that suffering can't be avoided, and if we never encountered it, there would be a lot of life lessons missed.

Grow in faith and trust.

Faith and trust are the antidotes to fear. I'm so glad that we can ask God to give us more faith when we feel we are lacking. When we stay close to the Lord and exercise the little faith we do have, He waters that seed of faith and makes it grow. When I focus on how God has been faithful to me in the past, I grow in trust.

It's been helpful for me to keep a prayer journal so that I can go back and see the ways God has rescued me and given me what I have needed countless times. When I read the Bible, I get to know God better, which helps me see that He is worthy of my trust. I won't trust someone I don't know. If we want to grow in trust, we have to take the time to get to know God personally.

Remember that I am never alone.

This comforts me most of all. Jesus has suffered more than I ever will, so He knows how I am feeling. The Bible promises that no matter what happens to me, God has made sure I can endure it (1 Corinthians 10:13). But He doesn't say I'll be able to handle anything in my own strength. I will have to cling to Him in order to receive the strength I need, just as a small branch clings to the main vine.

What is it that you most fear? Can you write it here?

Then write a prayer asking for God's help. You might want to affirm your trust in God's goodness and His control over all things, and thank Him for His wise plan for your life.

Dear God,

My Resolution

In what specific way will I apply what I have learned in this lesson?

1. When my fears are getting the better of me, I will make a Trust List. This is a list of ways in which I know I can trust God. It can contain words describing His character, or descriptions of times when He has proven to be faithful in the midst of my struggles. I'll reread this list (or make a new one) whenever I need a reminder.

2. I'll memorize one of the verses from this week's lesson. This will allow the Holy Spirit to bring it to my mind when I most need it.

3. I'll experience the shelter and safety of God's presence by spending some time this week at adoration.

My resolution:

Catechism Clip

CCC 227 [The implications of Faith in One God:] It means trusting God in every circumstance, even in adversity. A prayer of St. Teresa of Jesus wonderfully expresses this trust:

Let nothing trouble you / Let nothing frighten you
Everything passes / God never changes
Patience / Obtains all
Whoever has God / Wants for nothing
God alone is enough.

Appendix 1
SAINT THÉRÈSE OF LISIEUX

Patron Saint of Walking with Purpose

Saint Thérèse of Lisieux was gifted with the ability to take the riches of our Catholic faith and explain them in a way that a child could imitate. The wisdom she gleaned from Scripture ignited a love in her heart for her Lord that was personal and transforming. The simplicity of the faith that she laid out in her writings is so completely Catholic that Pope Pius XII said, "She rediscovered the Gospel itself, the very heart of the Gospel."

Walking with Purpose is intended to be a means by which women can honestly share their spiritual struggles and embark on a journey that is refreshing to the soul. It was never intended to facilitate the deepest of intellectual study of Scripture. Instead, the focus has been to help women know Christ: to know His heart, to know His tenderness, to know His mercy, and to know His love. Our logo is a little flower, and that has meaning. When a woman begins to open her heart to God, it's like the opening of a little flower. It can easily be bruised or crushed, and it must be treated with the greatest of care. Our desire is to speak to women's hearts no matter where they are in life, baggage and all, and gently introduce truths that can change their lives.

Saint Thérèse of Lisieux, the little flower, called her doctrine "the little way of spiritual childhood," and it is based on complete and unshakable confidence in God's love for us. She was not introducing new truths. She spent countless hours reading Scripture and she shared what she found, emphasizing the importance of truths that had already been divinely revealed. We can learn so much from her:

> The good God would not inspire unattainable desires; I can, then, in spite of my littleness, aspire to sanctity. For me to become greater is impossible; I must put up with myself just as I am with all my imperfections. But I wish to find the way to go to Heaven by a very straight, short, completely new little way. We are in a century of inventions: now one does not even have to take the trouble to climb the steps of a stairway; in the homes of the rich, an elevator replaces them nicely. I, too, would like to find an elevator to lift me up to Jesus, for I

am too little to climb the rough stairway of perfection. So I have looked in the books of the saints for a sign of the elevator I long for, and I have read these words proceeding from the mouth of eternal Wisdom: "He that is a little one, let him turn to me" (Proverbs 9:16). So I came, knowing that I had found what I was seeking, and wanting to know, O my God, what You would do with the little one who would answer Your call, and this is what I found:

"As one whom the mother caresses, so will I comfort you. You shall be carried at the breasts and upon the knees they shall caress you" (Isaiah 66:12–13). Never have more tender words come to make my soul rejoice. The elevator which must raise me to the heavens is Your arms, O Jesus! For that I do not need to grow; on the contrary, I must necessarily remain small, become smaller and smaller. O my God, You have surpassed what I expected, and I want to sing Your mercies. (Saint Thérèse of the Infant Jesus, *Histoire d'une Ame: Manuscrits Autobiographiques* [Paris: Éditions du Seuil, 1998], 244.)

Appendix 2
CONVERSION OF HEART

The Catholic faith is full of beautiful traditions, rituals, and sacraments. As powerful as they are, it is possible for them to become mere habits in our lives, instead of experiences that draw us close to the heart of Christ. In the words of John Paul II, they can become acts of "hollow ritualism." We might receive our first Communion and the sacraments of confession and confirmation, yet never experience the interior conversion that opens the heart to a personal relationship with God.

Pope Benedict XVI has explained that the "door of faith" is opened at one's baptism, but we are called to open it again, walk through it, and rediscover and renew our relationship with Christ and His Church.[18]

So how do we do this? How do we walk through that door of faith so we can begin to experience the abundant life that God has planned for us?

GETTING PERSONAL

The word *conversion* means "the act of turning." This means that conversion involves a turning away from one thing and a turning toward another. When you haven't experienced conversion of heart, you are turned *toward* your own desires. You are the one in charge, and you do what you feel is right and best at any given moment. You may choose to do things that are very good for other people, but the distinction is that *you are choosing*. You are deciding. You are the one in control.

Imagine driving a car. You are sitting in the driver's seat, and your hands are on the steering wheel. You've welcomed Jesus into the passenger's seat, and have listened to His comments. But whether or not you follow His directions is really up to you. You may follow them or you may not, depending on what seems right to you.

When you experience interior conversion, you decide to turn, to get out of the driver's seat, move into the passenger's seat, and invite God to be the driver. Instead of seeing Him as an advice giver or someone nice to have around for the holidays, you give Him control of every aspect of your life.

More than likely, you don't find this easy to do. This is because of the universal struggle with pride. We want to be the ones in charge. We don't like to be in desperate need. We like to be the captains of our ships, charting our own courses. As

---

[18] Pope Benedict XVI, *Apostolic Letter: Porta Fidei*, for the Indiction of the Year of Faith, October 11, 2011.

William Ernest Henley wrote, "I am the master of my fate: I am the captain of my soul."

Conversion of heart isn't possible without humility. The first step is to recognize your desperate need of a savior. Romans 6:23 states that the "wages of sin is death." When you hear this, you might be tempted to justify your behavior, or compare yourself with others. You might think to yourself, "I'm not a murderer. I'm not as bad as this or that person. If someone were to put my good deeds and bad deeds on a scale, my good ones would outweigh the bad. So surely I am good enough? Surely I don't deserve death!" When this is your line of thought, you are missing a very important truth: Just one sin is enough to separate you from a holy God. Just one sin is enough for you to deserve death. Even your best efforts to do good fall short of what God has required in order for you to spend eternity with Him. Isaiah 64:6 says, "All our righteous acts are like filthy rags." If you come to God thinking that you are going to be accepted by Him based on your "good conduct," He will point out that your righteousness is nothing compared to His infinite holiness.

Saint Thérèse of Lisieux understood this well, and wrote, "In the evening of my life I shall appear before You with empty hands, for I do not ask You to count my works. All our justices are stained in Your eyes. I want therefore to clothe myself in Your own justice and receive from Your love the eternal possession of Yourself."[19]

She recognized that her works, her best efforts, wouldn't be enough to earn salvation. Salvation cannot be earned. It's a free gift. Saint Thérèse accepted this gift, and said that if her justices or righteous deeds were stained, then she wanted to clothe herself in Christ's own justice. We see this described in 2 Corinthians 5:21: "God made him who had no sin to be sin for us, so that in him we might become the righteousness of God."

How did God make Him who had no sin to be sin for you? This was foretold by the prophet Isaiah: "But he was pierced for our transgressions, he was crushed for our iniquities; the punishment that brought us peace was upon him, and by his wounds we are healed." (Isaiah 53:5)

Jesus accomplished this on the cross. Every sin committed, past, present, and future, was placed on Him. Now, *all the merits of Jesus can be yours*. He wants to fill your empty hands with His own virtues.

But first, you need to recognize, just as Saint Thérèse did, that you are little. You are weak. You fail. You need forgiveness. You need a savior.

---

[19] Saint Thérèse of Lisieux, "Act of Oblation to Merciful Love," June 9, 1895.

When you come before God in prayer and acknowledge these truths, He looks at your heart. He sees your desire to trust Him, to please Him, to obey Him. He says to you, "My precious child, you don't have to pay for your sins. My Son, Jesus, has already done that for you. He suffered, so that you wouldn't have to. I want to experience a relationship of intimacy with you. I forgive you.[20] Jesus came to set you free.[21] When you open your heart to me, you become a new creation![22] The old you has gone. The new you is here. If you will stay close to me, and journey by my side, you will begin to experience a transformation that brings joy and freedom.[23] I've been waiting to pour my gifts into your soul. Beloved daughter of mine, remain confident in me. I am your loving Father. Crawl into my lap. Trust me. Love me. I will take care of everything."

This is conversion of heart. This act of faith lifts the veil from your eyes and launches you into the richest and most satisfying life. You don't have to be sitting in church to do this. Don't let a minute pass before opening your heart to God and inviting Him to come dwell within you. Let Him sit in the driver's seat. Give Him the keys to your heart. Your life will never be the same again.

---

[20] "If we acknowledge our sins, he is faithful and just and will forgive our sins and cleanse us from every wrongdoing." 1 John 1:9

[21] "So if the Son makes you free, you will be free indeed." John 8:36

[22] "So whoever is in Christ is a new creation: the old things have passed away; behold, new things have come." 2 Corinthians 5:18

[23] "I will sprinkle clean water over you to make you clean; from all your impurities and from all your idols I will cleanse you. I will give you a new heart, and a new spirit I will put within you. I will remove the heart of stone from your flesh and give you a heart of flesh." Ezekiel 36:25, 26

Appendix 3
ANSWER KEY

Lesson 1, Day One

1. **A.** Answers will vary.
   B. The psalmist saw the hand of God creating him, intentionally forming him into a wonderful, known person. He saw God caring about each detail of his life, shaping his days even before he was born. He considered himself wonderfully made—a one-of-a-kind work of art.

2. **A.** People judge based on appearance and status, but God is different. He looks deep within us—He looks at our hearts.
   B. Answers will vary.

3. **A.** Jesus did not save us because of righteous deeds we have done. He saved us because He is kind, generous, and merciful.
   B. He saved us through the bath of rebirth and renewal by the Holy Spirit (the sacrament of baptism), which was poured out on us. He saved us so that we could be justified by His grace and become heirs in hopes of eternal life.
   C. We were saved while we were still sinners.

4. **A.** Through faith and baptism, we are now children of God.
   B. God sent the Holy Spirit to live in us to prove that we are His children. We are to call God our Abba—our daddy.

5. We can be led by the Spirit of God. This is not a spirit that causes us to fall back into fear, but one of adoption, that allows us to cry, "Abba, Father!" The Holy Spirit testifies with our spirit that we are children of God.

Lesson 1, Day Two

1. **A.** Answers will vary.
   B. In this verse, Jesus tells us that it wasn't a matter of us choosing Him. *He* has chosen *us*. He wants us.

2. We are to guard our hearts.

3. **Song of Songs 4:7** "You are beautiful in every way, my friend, there is no flaw in you!"
   Isaiah 41:10 "Do not fear; I am with you; do not be anxious; I am your God. I will strengthen you, I will help you, I will uphold you with my victorious right hand."
   Isaiah 43:4 "Because you are precious in my eyes and honored, and I love you, I give people in return for you and nations in exchange for your life."
   Isaiah 49:15–16 "Can a mother forget her infant, be without tenderness for the child of her womb? Even should she forget, I will never forget you. See, upon the palms of my hands I have engraved you; your walls are ever before me."
   Psalm 34:8 "The angel of the Lord encamps around those who fear him, and he saves them."
   Psalm 56:9 "My wanderings you have noticed; are my tears not stored in your flask, recorded in your book?"
   Exodus 14:14 "The Lord will fight for you; you have only to keep still."
   1 Corinthians 1:27–29 "God chose the foolish of the world to shame the wise, and God chose the weak of the world to shame the strong, and God chose the lowly and despised of the world, those who count for nothing, to reduce to nothing those who are something, so that no human being might boast before God."
   John 14:1–3 "Do not let your hearts be troubled. You have faith in God; have faith also in me. In my Father's house there are many dwelling places. If there were not, would I have told you

that I am going to prepare a place for you? And if I go and prepare a place for you, I will come back again and take you to myself, so that where I am you also may be."

Lesson 1, Day Three

1. **A.** These verses tell us to be on our guard, to stand firm in the faith, to be courageous, and to be strong.
   B. Answers will vary.
2. Answers will vary.
3. **A.** According to Philippians 3:20, our citizenship is in heaven.
   B. That community is described as a "great cloud of witnesses."
   C. The great cloud of witnesses is watching us run the race that lies before us.
   D. Answers will vary.

Lesson 1, Day Four

1. **A.** Jesus tells us that we aren't to worry about what we eat, drink, or wear. God knows what we need. We're told to seek *first* the kingdom of God and His righteousness, and then all the things we need will be given to us.
   B. Answers will vary.
2. Answers will vary.
3. **Matthew 6:24–25** Jesus said that if we are going to be His followers, we must deny ourselves and take up our cross. If we lose our life in the worldly sense, we'll actually gain it eternally.
   John 12:24-25 Just as a grain of wheat "dies" when it's buried in the ground, but then bears fruit, our little deaths, our sacrifices, produce fruit as well.
   Philippians 3:8 Saint Paul considered all earthly gains to be rubbish in comparison to the surpassing value of knowing Christ.
4. **A.** Answers will vary.
   B. Answers will vary.

Lesson 2, Day One

1. Peter took his eyes off of Jesus and focused on the waves. He was saved from drowning because Jesus reached out His hand and caught him.
2. He's given us a spirit of power, love, and self-control.
3. Answers will vary.

Lesson 2, Day Two

No. Jesus said that in this world we'll actually have trouble. But He encouraged us to take heart, because He has overcome the world.
2. She learned that everything passes; our troubles have an end date. Only God never changes. If we are patient in our difficulties, we'll learn that God alone is enough.
3. **A.** We don't walk alone. This passage encourages us to be strong and steadfast; to have no fear, for it is the Lord, our God, who marches with us; He will never fail us or forsake us.
   B. In Jesus' presence, we are never in darkness. He is our light and He promises to save us. Because He is with us, we don't need to be afraid.
   C. God is always with us. He promises to always strengthen and uphold us.
   D. Nothing can separate us from the love of God. Nothing.
4. Answers will vary.

Lesson 2, Day Three

1. It's described as a snare.

2. **Romans 8:31** Ultimately, it's only God's opinion that matters. And the Creator of the universe is *for us*.

   Galatians 1:10 We have a choice. We can either seek to please people or seek to please God. We can't have it both ways.

   Colossians 3:23 Whatever we do, our motive for doing it should be to please God, not to try to meet the expectations of people around us.
3. Answers will vary.

Lesson 2, Day Four
1. **John 10:10** It's described as an abundant life.

   1 Timothy 6:17 It's described as a life in which all the things God has provided for us are for our enjoyment.

   Isaiah 30:18 It's described as a life in which the Lord is waiting to be gracious to us, to show us mercy.
2. Answers will vary.
3. Answers will vary.

NOTES

No program near you? No problem...it's easy to start your own group in your parish or at home and we will walk with you every step of the way. Find out more:

www.walkingwithpurpose.com/leadership

"See to it that no one misses the grace of God" Hebrews 12:15

It's time to stop talking about how there's nothing relevant out there for Catholic women.

IT'S TIME TO BE THE CHANGE WE WANT TO SEE.

You can bring **Walking with Purpose** to your parish!

IT'S EASY TO DO!

You've already got the skills needed!
- Personal commitment to Christ
- Desire to share the love of Christ
- Belief in the power of authentic, transparent community

We'll be there every step of the way, offering:
- Training
- Mentoring
- Bible study materials
- Promotional materials

Do you think you have too many limitations to serve in this way?

Great! That's *exactly* where God wants us to start. If we will just offer Him *what we have*, He promises to do the rest. Few things stretch and grow our faith like stepping out and asking God to work through us. Say *YES*, and get ready to watch what He can do through imperfect women who depend on Him.

Learn more about bringing **Walking with Purpose** to your parish!

Visit us at **walkingwithpurpose.com**

walking with purpose

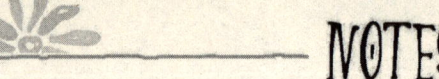

NOTES

"For to the one who has, more will be given"
Matthew 13:12

THANK YOU

for sharing this journey with all of us at **Walking with Purpose**.
We'd love to stay connected!
We've got more encouragement and hope available for you!

FREE valuable resources:

- Print out or download WWP Scripture Verses, can also be used as lock screens for phones.

- Join our community on Facebook, Twitter, Pinterest and Instagram for a daily boost!

- Subscribe to our Blog for regular inspiration and participate in conversations by contributing your comments!

The Walking with Purpose Bible study program is just the beginning.

Go to **walkingwithpurpose.com** to subscribe to our Blog and connect with us on Social Media

walking with purpose

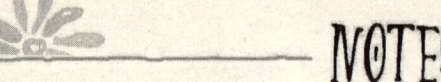

NOTES

THE OPENING YOUR HEART SERIES

Beloved: *Opening Your Heart, Part I,* is a six-lesson Bible study that lays a strong foundation for our true identity as beloved daughters of God.

Unshaken: *Opening Your Heart, Part II,* is a six-lesson Bible study that fills our spiritual toolbox with exactly what we need to grow stronger in our faith.

Steadfast: *Opening Your Heart, Part III,* a six-lesson Bible study, unpacks why we are hustling for our worth and how to conquer our fears.

THE KEEPING IN BALANCE SERIES

Harmony: Keeping in Balance, Part I
Perspective: Keeping in Balance, Part II
Exhale: Keeping in Balance, Part III

THE DISCOVERING OUR DIGNITY SERIES

Tapestry: Discovering Our Dignity, Part I
Legacy: Discovering our Dignity, Part II
Heritage: Discovering Our Dignity, Part III

For more information on all Walking with Purpose Bible studies please visit us at
walkingwithpurpose.com

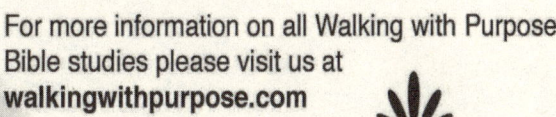

walking with purpose

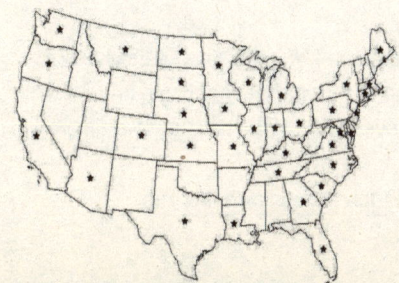

Walking with Purpose is a community of women growing in faith – together! This is where women are gathering. Join us!

www.walkingwithpurpose.com/find-program-near

No program near you? No problem...it's easy to start your own group in your parish or at home and we will walk with you every step of the way. Find out more:

www.walkingwithpurpose.com/leadership